W9-ADB-388

THE ITALIAN-KOSHER COOKBOOK

 BY RUTH AND BOB GROSSMAN

GALAHAD BOOKS · NEW YORK CITY

Published by Galahad Books, a division of A & W Promo-
tional Book Corporation, 95 Madison Avenue, New York,
N.Y. 10016, by arrangement with Paul S. Eriksson, Inc.,
119 West 57th Street, New York, N.Y. 10019.

Library of Congress Catalog Card No.: 73-81654
ISBN: 0-88365-085-1

Copyright © 1964 by Ruth and Bob Grossman. All rights
reserved. No part of this book may be reproduced in any
form without permission of the publisher.

Manufactured in the United States of America.

THE ITALIAN-KOSHER COOKBOOK

By the same authors

THE CHINESE-KOSHER COOKBOOK

To the ladies of Hadassah,
God bless them, every one!

All recipes in this book have been authenticated as Kosher by Rabbi Norman Siegel of the Jewish Center of Kings Highway, Brooklyn, New York.

Thou shalt not eat any abominable thing . . .

And every beast that parteth the hoof, and cleaveth the cleft into two claws, and chewest the cud among beasts, that ye shall eat . . .

These ye shall eat of all that are in the waters: all that have fins and scales shall ye eat . . .

Of all clean birds ye shall eat . . .

But these are they of which ye shall not eat: the eagle, the ossifrage and the osprey . . . and the glede, and the kite, and the vulture after his kind,

And every raven after his kind . . .

And every creeping thing that flieth is unclean unto you: they shall not be eaten . . .

But of all clean fowls ye may eat . . .

Ye shall not eat of any thing that dieth of itself . . . thou shalt not seethe a kid in his mother's milk . . .

DEUTERONOMY XIV

*To the ladies of Hadassah,
God bless them, every one!*

All recipes in this book have been authenticated as Kosher by Rabbi Norman Siegel of the Jewish Center of Kings Highway, Brooklyn, New York.

Thou shalt not eat any abominable thing . . .

And every beast that parteth the hoof, and cleaveth the cleft into two claws, and chewest the cud among beasts, that ye shall eat . . .

These ye shall eat of all that are in the waters: all that have fins and scales shall ye eat . . .

Of all clean birds ye shall eat . . .

But these are they of which ye shall not eat: the eagle, the ossifrage and the osprey . . . and the glede, and the kite, and the vulture after his kind,

And every raven after his kind . . .

And every creeping thing that flieth is unclean unto you: they shall not be eaten . . .

But of all clean fowls ye may eat . . .

Ye shall not eat of any thing that dieth of itself . . . thou shalt not seethe a kid in his mother's milk . . .

DEUTERONOMY XIV

PREFACE

It wasn't too many years ago that Grandma Slipakoff stunned the whole family with her tradition breaking Kosher Chinese recipes . . . . not only the family—the neighbors, and even friends thought this "Chinese kick" would pass. Grandma knew her traditional Kosher dishes were no longer interesting enough to lure "the kids" back home every Friday night.

But Grandma started going overboard. How much Kosher Chinese food can a person eat? EGG ROLL HAH DAH SAH or CHICKEN GOY YIM WITH VEGETABLES are really great, now and then. Even FAH SHTUNK KEN NAH FISH ROLL is a real treat, occasionally. And how often can you eat FAR BLUN JED EGG DROP SOUP?

Then Grandma noticed we started drifting away again. When she'd call us, it was usually, "Noo? So what's the matter? Mine Chinese Kosher cooking's not good enough? You were wanting maybe SHLUMAZOL STUFFED ARTICHOKE?"

This could mean only one thing! Grandma was now involved in

another major campaign . . . this time collecting *Italian* recipes and making them Kosher, so she could present to the family a whole new menu of gourmet delights from which to choose. So, we pulled out the note paper and thought—here we go again! These recipes, just as the Chinese Kosher ones, must be preserved for posterity . . . we have to write another cookbook!

Grandma now actually makes her own spaghetti, except on Shabbos, of course, when she can't cook and we all sit around eating AH BISSEL BORSHT MILANESE.

It's pretty hard these days to hide a smile when she pulls out her own special *espresso* coffee maker . . . . and she's quite proud of her new culinary achievements. We're back in the fold again; and Grandma, happy in her new role of Creator of Kosher Foods of all Nations, is now trying to get Manischewitz to put out "a nice Chianti, it should be dry."

Ruth & Bob Grossman

Brooklyn Heights, N. Y.

TABLE OF ❦ CONTENTS

THE ITALIAN-KOSHER COOKBOOK

SO YOU THINK IT'S ALL SPAGHETTI!

If you ask most people, they'll say that Italian food is pasta, tomato sauce, oregano and garlic. They're right . . . but, there's more to it than that. There are nice veal dishes, chicken fixed all kinds ways, polenta (this is a cornmeal mush they like in Northern Italy), lots of good, healthy vegetables, fish, and even rice sometimes instead of spaghetti. But since most Italian restaurants are run by immigrants from Sicily and Southern Italy, the Italian foods most Americans know are heavy with tomato and meat sauces, Parmesan cheese on almost everything, and all kinds pizza pies and plenty olive oil.

The food in Northern Italy is not so heavy as in Southern Italy. But everywhere they have their favorite pastas, olive oil and such spices! In the North, they're mostly using butter, instead of olive oil—with meat yet! So we're using *parve* oleomargerine where they're using butter. . . .

Some people think Italian food is loaded with garlic. Look, Italians are like everybody else . . . they have things "that just don't agree with me," too. Some like lots of garlic, and some don't. It's better to have not enough than too much anyway. If you're serving garlic to company, just be sure everyone eats it. That way, nobody is offended . . . nobody is offensive.

In Italy they're using wine, but it's not exactly Kosher. In these recipes, you'll find sometimes red, sometimes white wine . . . but always the wines were Kosher, and put out by nice people who really know the Kosher wine business. If you ever go through one of their wineries, it'll take you maybe a few days to sober up . . . but, believe me, when it's all over you'll be a *mayvin* of Kosher wines! *Better you should remember some of these cooking hints:*

In New York there is a manufacturer who makes strictly Kosher Ricotta and Mozzarella cheeses. However, if you can't get these Kosher cheeses in your city, cottage cheese is just like Ricotta, and Muenster cheese melts just like Mozzarella.

If you're using canned tomatoes, you'll put them in a blender and

1

give a few quick blends . . . otherwise, break up with the fork to take out from them the lumps. If you're using fresh tomatoes, put them in boiling water for about 30 seconds. Then peel them and dice them. Use very red, ripe tomatoes. It'll give the sauce such a nice rich color.

When you use capers in your cooking, and if you buy the kind that comes packed in vinegar, you'll be sure to rinse off the capers to remove the extra vinegar. If the capers are for salad or antipasto, why rinse?

Veal cutlets, buy sliced very thin. If the butcher's a nice *haymisha* man, he'll pound them for you, or you can pound yourself with a mallet or even the bottom of a heavy pot.

When you're cooking spaghetti or other pasta, add a tiny splash oil to the cooking water. This way it doesn't all stick together and make such a mess! And you don't have to rinse off with cold water, which —what else?—makes cold the spaghetti.

Don't ever break the spaghetti when you're boiling it, or the lasagne or any long pasta. If your pot seems too small, put part of the pasta in the water, and little by little you'll push with a spoon the rest of it. As it softens, it bends . . . like magic. You shouldn't be embarrassed to twirl long spaghetti on your fork. Just look around and you'll find everyone else is doing it, too. The secret is, you shouldn't start with too much spaghetti. Just don't slurp (not too loud anyway). At least spaghetti is a lot easier than fighting chopsticks!

When cooking sauces, it's better to have a nice heavy bottomed pot. This way the heat is even and there's not so much chance your sauce will stick to your bottom. But now and then you should stir. Stirring is very good for people who don't smoke anymore . . . . and need to do something with their hands. All this and the sauce doesn't stick either!

Italians drink wine the way we drink seltzer . . . . and a meal's not a meal unless you have a nice dry wine. You don't have to get *shicker* at every meal; just have enough in a wine glass to put that nice little touch.

And, finally, there's something about candlelight that makes a delicious Italian meal even better yet. That, plus a glass wine, and maybe a little soft music on the hi-fi, and oy, vay! don't ask!

ANTIPASTO

ANTIPASTO*

Every Italian restaurant has antipasto on the menu. This can be everything from lettuce, pimiento, sardines & different kinds sausages and cheese (such a combination you shouldn't know from it!) to stuffed mushrooms, stuffed eggplants, some kind of *hahzarei* they call clams, and lots other stuff. Every restaurant has its own special antipasto . . . some good; some not so good. And over the whole thing you usually pour oil and vinegar. On the next page are suggestions for an antipasto to serve whether you're having *fleischig* or *milchig*. You can use your imagination to add all sorts of other interesting specialties you may have:

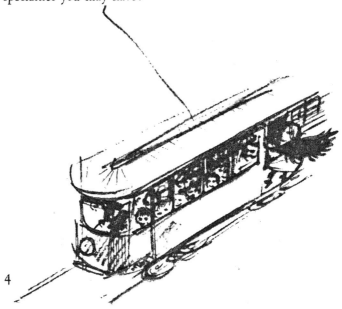

4

ANTIPASTO FLEISCHIG

In the list you see here, some things you can get out of a can or at the nearest delicatessen. The ones with asterisks you'll find recipes for on the next few pages.

Cocktail frankfurters
Corned beef slices
Pastrami slices
**Eggs Diablo Alla Tuhmel
Olives (black & green)
Pimiento
Kosher Pickle
Eggplant (comes in jars with vinegar)

**Pickled Mushrooms Facrimta Puhnum
Very thinly sliced corned beef around a wedge of honeydew melon
Parsley sprigs
Chick Peas

ANTIPASTO MILCHIG

You used to call it "tonight we're having dairy." But when you're using this book, it becomes Antipasto Milchig. For this we suggest:

Cheese slices (many varieties)
Soft cheeses
Various smoked fish
Sardines
Anchovies
Olives (black & green)

Pimiento
Eggs stuffed with tuna fish
Celery
Cherry tomatoes
Scallions

* *ANTIPASTO:* what the Italians serve in place of chopped liver.

5

 EGGS DIABLO ALLA TUHMEL*

6 hard-boiled eggs	2 small cloves garlic, mashed
2 teaspoons wine vinegar	1 teaspoon salt
1½ tablespoons olive oil	Dash pepper

Cut each egg in half and take out from the whites the yolks, and mash them together with everything else. Now put back into the whites, the yolks . . . but be careful you don't tear the whites . . . an artist you should be in the kitchen.

* TUHMEL: the family reaction when Steve announced he was getting his own apartment.

6

PICKLED MUSHROOMS
FACRIMTA PUHNUM*

1 lb. button mushrooms	1 teaspoon mustard seed
1½ cups wine vinegar	1 teaspoon peppercorns
½ cup water	A few pinches salt
1 teaspoon celery seed	¼ cup olive oil

A few cloves garlic

In a saucepan, you should simmer nice everything but the mushrooms. After 5 minutes of simmering, throw in the mushrooms and for another 5 minutes you'll simmer. Then you can pack good the mushrooms into a sterilized jar and pour in the liquid. If you don't have enough liquid left, it's alright to add a little bit water. Cover the jar tight and put it in a cool place for at least 2 days before you'll serve. This is not only good to use in an antipasto, but it's also good to put in a tossed salad for a little extra *tamm*.

* *FACRIMTA PUHNUM:* Mom's description of the girl who jilted her son, Herbie.

CAPONATA MESHUGENUH PAPPARAZZI*

2 medium eggplants	2 ounces capers, drained
1½ cups olive oil	2 tablespoons sugar
2 nice size onions, sliced	¼ cup wine vinegar
1¼ cups canned tomatoes, drained	A few pinches salt & pepper

First wash nice the eggplants and cut up into small cubes. Then you can fry in the oil until they are soft and a little brown. When they are done, take them out from the pan and drain. Then you can fry nice the onions until they are soft and golden. Put the eggplants and onions in a bowl and throw in the tomatoes and capers. Chop this up a little so there are no big chunks left. Now this whole mess you'll put already into a saucepan, mix together the vinegar and sugar and pour this also in. Add the salt and pepper and let it simmer on the fire for about 20 minutes. Every once in a while make sure to give a stir. Now let it get good and cold. This is a wonderful shmear for crackers at a party, and it's also good when it's part of an antipasto. What you don't use up right away, you'll put in the refrigerator. It keeps for days. Serve this in large amounts, because with this people make from themselves real pigs (you should pardon the expression!)

* *MESHUGENUH PAPPARAZZI*: those crazy Italian photographers who are busy chasing after Italian actresses when they could be photographing some nice Jewish girls.

ARTICHOKES JUDAEA
COHN MITZVAH*

As many artichokes as you
need to make 1 per person
A little lemon juice

A pot hot oil
A little salt & pepper

Tell your vegetable man to pick out small and tender artichokes. When you get home, cut off from them the first half inch of the tips and peel nice the stems. Also, you can take off all the tough outside leaves. Now pour a little lemon juice into some water and wash the artichokes in this. After you wash, you'll turn upside down so they'll drain good. (It's a good idea to do this a few hours before you fry. If there's any water left on the artichokes, when you fry, the pot will boil over and make from your kitchen a mess!)

Now make the oil good and hot and fry a few artichokes at a time until they're a nice golden brown. Let them drain and sprinkle with a little salt and pepper. If you like potato chips, you'll like this. This dish is very popular with the Jews in Rome and it's about time everybody knew about it. This everyone will love . . . . . but serve as soon as they're cooked, and don't forget to eat the heart.

* *MITZVAH:* when Sam Cohn donated his Christmas bonus to the *shul.*

SHLUMAZEL STUFFED
ARTICHOKE*

This recipe is just for 1 artichoke, but who ever heard of cooking just one? So what you'll do is multiply each amount of the ingredients by the number of artichokes you want to fix. All you'll need is 1 artichoke for each person.

¼ cup bread crumbs
¼ cup grated Parmesan cheese
1 small clove garlic, minced
1 tablespoon fine chopped onions
1 tablespoon chopped parsley

1 teaspoon olive oil
3 tablespoons vegetable broth
A few pinches salt and pepper
A nice dash paprika
1 artichoke

First you should mix together the bread crumbs, cheese, garlic, onions, parsley, olive oil, broth, salt and pepper and paprika. Put this aside and start fixing up the artichokes. Cut off from the tip the first half inch, then cut off the stem, peel off the tough outside leaves, and cut out the choke from the inside. (That's the hairy part.) Now push down the artichoke on the table top so the leaves will spread out a little. The stuffing you should put in the center of the artichoke, although some folks stuff it in between the leaves. You do the way you like best. Now you'll put the artichoke into a saucepan and put in about an inch of water and a pinch salt. Put on tight the cover and let it steam for a half hour or so. It's ready when you can pull out from it easy, a leaf. You can serve artichokes hot or cold, they're so good. When you eat this, be sure to serve knives and don't forget to eat the heart . . . . it's the best part! You'll need extra napkins with this.

---

* SHLUMAZEL: describes the fellow who when told, "Sorry, next elevator!" answers, "That's the story of my life."

PRESSED TUNA ALLA GANTZE MISHPOKHE*

1-7 oz. can salmon
3-7 oz. cans tuna
¼ lb. butter, melted
3 nice fresh beaten eggs

A few good pinches pepper
2 tablespoon chopped parsley
¼ cup drained capers
¼ cup shelled pistachio nuts

Remove first the skins and bones from the can salmon. Now mix it together with the tuna and chop it up, it should be fine. Next you'll mix in the butter, eggs, pepper, parsley and capers. With an electric mixer you should mix for a few minutes so everything is together nice. Then you can throw in the pistachio nuts and mix a little more. Grease good the top part of a double boiler and make in it a lining from wax paper. In this the tuna mish-mash should go. Cook for an hour, and let it cool. While it's cooling you should lay on the top of the tuna a small plate and on this put something heavy, so that the mixture will get pressed good. Put the double boiler top (be sure it's cooled enough) with the weights in the refrigerator to chill. When you're ready to serve, take off from the top the plate and the weights and put the double boiler top in hot water for a few minutes. Now you can take it out. On a plate you'll turn it upside down, and let the pressed tuna fall out. One thing you shouldn't forget, peel off the wax paper before you serve. And maybe you can give a little squeeze of lemon juice on top. This makes more than enough to serve for Mah Jong or Bocci or whatever the girls play.

* GANTZE MISHPOKHE: the family Board of Directors who tell you what you want to be when you grow up, and with whom!

STUFFED EGGPLANT
INDIGESTIONE*

1 small eggplant
1 small onion, chopped
1 clove garlic, minced
1 teaspoon oregano
2 tablespoons olive oil
A few pinches salt

½ cup bread crumbs
1 beaten egg
A little chopped parsley
A little grated Parmesan
cheese

Bake first the eggplant in a medium oven for 30 minutes or until it looks like somebody let the air out from it. Then you can cut it into 4 wedges and scoop out from it, the insides. Don't forget to save the skins. Now you can sauté the onion, garlic and oregano in 1 tablespoon of the oil until they get soft. Mix this together with the eggplant insides (make sure there are no lumps), the salt and the bread crumbs. Then you can add the beaten egg and the other tablespoon oil. Mix together nice and stuff into the eggplant skins. On top you can sprinkle a little of the chopped parsley and Parmesan cheese. Put them under the broiler for 10 or 15 minutes and they're done. Makes enough for 3 or 4 people, they should have hearty appetites!

* *INDIGESTIONE*: the Italian answer to Jewish heartburn.

STUFFED MUSHROOMS
ALLA MOHEL*

1 tablespoon anise seed	½ cup melted oleo
½ cup water	A little splash hot sauce
1 tight packed cup spinach	A nice pinch salt
¼ cup also tight parsley	3 anchovies, mashed
1 medium onion	½ cup bread crumbs

About 2 dozen nice mushroom caps

Simmer first the anise seed in the water for 10 minutes, then throw away the seeds and keep the water. In a blender add the anise seed water, the spinach, parsley, onion and melted oleo. Blend it all together so it should be smooth. Now mix in the hot sauce, salt, and smashed anchovies. Put this in a little saucepan and simmer for 10 or 12 minutes. Afterwards, you'll throw in the bread crumbs. When it's mixed nice together, heap up good in each mushroom cap some of the stuffing and put them under the broiler for 10 to 15 minutes. Serve it hot to your guests and, believe me, they'll lick their fingers. (Better that, than wipe them on your tablecloth.)

* *MOHEL:* a surgeon who performs only at parties.

KOKKAPITZZI PIZZA WITH LOX*

YOU NEED A NICE DOUGH:

1 package yeast	2 tablespoons oil
⅞ cup water, warmed	2⅔ cups flour, sifted

A pinch salt

First you'll add the yeast to the warm water and let it soften. Then add the salt, oil and flour. Knead for 5 minutes until it gets smooth and a little rubbery, and you get a little tired. Brush it with a little oil and put it in a bowl. Cover the bowl with a cloth and let it stand in a warm place, like maybe by the radiator, for about 2 hours until the dough gets twice as big.

MEANWHILE, YOU'LL MAKE THE SAUCE:

2 tablespoons oil	1 cup water
2 medium onions, chopped fine	Salt and pepper, enough to taste
1-6 oz. can tomato paste	

Sauté good the onions for about 5 minutes. Then you'll add the tomato paste and the water. Also the salt and pepper. Let this simmer uncovered 15 minutes, while you sit and have a sip of coffee.

14

NOW FOR THE OTHER STUFF:

1 tablespoon olive oil	½ cup lox in shreds
1 cup Mozzarella cheese, sliced thin	A little oregano

When the dough has grown to double its size, you can knead it again on a floury board and spread it out into a large 14 inch circle. Now take a 14 or 15 inch flat pan and smear on it a little olive oil. Spread out the dough in the pan and put plenty of the sauce on it, you should cover all over. Now put on the tablespoon olive oil and sprinkle on the Mozzarella. Put on the pieces lox (you can also use mushrooms and/or anchovies) and sprinkle on the oregano. Now you can put the whole thing into a 500° oven and let it bake for 15 or 20 minutes until the edges turn a little brown and the cheese is bubbling. Slice it up in wedges and serve. If you want that real pizzeria atmosphere, the only way to do it is buy a jukebox and invite lots of teen-agers; but, believe me, pizza with lox they won't find at the neighborhood Pizza Palace!

* KOKKAPITZZI: a Southern Yiddish word meaning everything but the kitchen stove, which is optional.

LEONARDO DA VINCI
GARLIC BREAD*

1 long loaf Italian bread	Salt & pepper, 'til it tastes
2 cloves garlic, minced	like something
½ cup olive oil	Maybe a sprinkle paprika
	for color

In a saucepan, warm up the olive oil and the garlic and salt and pepper. Now you'll cut the bread like you're going to slice it, only don't cut all the way. (Later you'll see how easy it'll be to tear off each slice.) Now shmear the heated mixture in each slit, sprinkle on the paprika, and wrap the whole loaf in foil and put it in the oven. If you're cooking other things in the oven and it's very hot, the bread should be done in no time at all. Just keep an eye on it. But if you check it, use a thick potholder so you don't get burned from the heat. Otherwise, cook at 375° about 15 minutes. Tonight you'll be generous with the garlic . . . tomorrow, the mouthwash!

* *LEONARDO DA VINCI:* "my son the painter, the mathematician, the mechanic, the inventor, the anatomist, the sculptor, the scientist, the architect, the engineer. . . . . . ."

16

SOUPS

MINESTRONE DELLA CONTESSA GOLDFARB*

2 tablespoons olive oil
2 nice onions, chopped
2 quarts meat stock
1 cup cut up string beans
2 tablespoons tomato paste
1 nice handful spinach, torn up
1 tablespoon parsley, chopped
2 chopped up carrots
1 can kidney beans
2 small zucchini, sliced
2 medium potatoes, diced
¼ small cabbage, shredded
Enough salt & pepper so it will have a taste
1 tablespoon MSG
1 cup Tubettini (Macaroni #42)
A little extra stock to pour in, if you need

Put in a nice big pot the oil and sauté the onions until they get soft. Then the meat stock you can throw in (if you made flanken more often, then maybe you'd have meat stock) and then the rest of the ingredients, but not the Tubettini. Cover the pot and let it cook for ½ hour. Now you can throw in the Tubettini and a little more stock if the soup is too thick. Let it cook for another 20 minutes and it's ready to serve to an army. But don't worry, it keeps nice in the refrigerator. Serves 1 Army.

* LA CONTESSA GOLDFARB: the Italian Jennie Grossinger.

AH BISSEL BORSHT MILANESE*

10 medium sized beets	½ teaspoon pepper
10 cups vegetable bouillon	1 tablespoon sugar
4 ripe tomatoes, peeled & diced	1 cup cream
1 tablespoon lemon juice	¼ cup flour
1 tablespoon salt	2 eggs

Wash, peel and slice nice the beets. Put the bouillon and beets in a large pot, cover and bring to a boil. Make low the heat, and simmer until the beets are nice and tender and everything good has been cooked out of them. Meantime, you'll put the tomatoes in a blender with lemon juice, salt, pepper, sugar, the sour cream and flour. When it's all blended nice so there are no lumps in the mish-mash, pour it slowly into the soup, stirring constantly. Now you'll cool it. Some people like it hot; but to most people, there's no borsht like cold borsht. When the soup is cooled, you should blend in slowly the eggs. This will be the most unusual borsht you ever had . . . who ever heard of borsht with tomatoes in it? But listen, who ever heard of an Italian-Kosher Cookbook? This makes a pot that'll serve the family for days. With all the beets that are left over, you can serve them as a vegetable with a little margerine or you can marinate them, in vinegar and pickling spices.

* AH BISSEL BORSHT: what Mrs. Michelangelo put in her son's thermos everyday when he was working at the Sistine Chapel.

MAMA LEVY'S VENDETTA
LENTIL SOUP*

3 quarts water	1 cup canned tomatoes
1 lb. lentils	A few pinches salt & pepper,
3 tablespoons olive oil	to taste
1 clove garlic, minced	A few sprinkles Parmesan
1 onion, chopped	cheese
1 stalk celery, diced	

Cook the lentils in 3 quarts boiling water for about 1 hour and 15 minutes. While this is cooking, you'll brown lightly in olive oil the garlic, onion and celery. When the lentils are through cooking, strain them through a sieve with the tomatoes. Add now a cup of water or enough to make the soup as thick or as thin as you like it and the salt and pepper. Then put in the garlic, onion and celery and simmer for 10 minutes. When you serve the soup, you can sprinkle a little cheese on top (depending what the rest of the meal is). This makes enough for 6 people, with some left over for a nice nosh for tomorrow.

* *MAMA LEVY'S VENDETTA*: wait 'til your father comes home —then you'll get it!

ZUPPA DI ESCAROLE
GOYISHA KUPP*

6 cups nice chicken soup	1 chopped onion
2 tablespoons tomato paste	1 chopped carrot
2 teaspoons salt	1 cup diced celery
A little bit pepper	2 cups pasta shells
4 cups shredded escarole	

Mix everything together in a nice soup pot, except the pasta shells and the escarole, and simmer for about a half hour. Now bring to a boil and add the shells and escarole and continue cooking until the shells are done. Take one of the shells and give a little chew to see if it's tender . . . it takes about 15 minutes. And, believe it or not, that's all there is to it. You'll have to decide for yourself how many it serves, because everybody's soup bowls are different.

* *GOYISHA KUPP*: he thinks a "shofar" is someone who drives a Rolls Royce.

SALADS & DRESSINGS

SHNORRA STRING BEAN SALAD*

6 tablespoons olive oil
3 tablespoons wine vinegar
A few pinches salt & pepper
1 chopped onion

1 lb. string beans, cooked & drained
4 hard-boiled eggs, chopped
3 tablespoons mayonnaise

1 teaspoon prepared mustard

Anyone can make easily this dish. It's mostly just mixing different things together. You mix the olive oil, wine vinegar, salt and pepper, and onion. Then add all this to the drained string beans and chill awhile. When you take it out from the refrigerator, you'll mix (again with the mixing!) the chopped eggs with mayonnaise and mustard. A drop of vinegar in this adds a nice *tamm*. Cover this egg mixture and chill it. When it's ready to serve, you'll spoon the string bean mixture on plates covered with lettuce, and on top of this you'll put the egg mixture. If company's coming over, this can be finished even before they ring the doorbell. It's enough for 4 salads. If you're having more, you'll fix more.

* *SHNORRA*: sees his dentist twice a year to read all the magazines he "can't afford."

 EXCITING DRESSINGS SO YOU
SHOULDN'T SERVE NEBISH
SALADS*

ANCHOVY DRESSING

4 anchovies	3 tablespoons wine vinegar
½ cup olive oil	A little pepper

Mash the anchovies to a paste . . . don't cheat . . . . . be sure it's very mashed. Then you'll add the rest of the ingredients and mix everything all up.

ITALIAN CHEESE DRESSING

¼ cup olive oil	A few pinches salt &
3 tablespoons wine vinegar	pepper
	¼ cup grated cheese

You'll mix nice all the ingredients and blend it very good. Better you should put a sticker on it saying "Cheese" or you might make a very embarrassing mistake.

OIL AND VINEGAR DRESSING

⅓ cup wine vinegar
1 clove garlic, mashed
6 tablespoons olive oil

A little salt & pepper
A couple pinches oregano

Put this all in a jar or bottle and give a few healthy shakes. Let it stand overnight in the refrigerator, then the next day you've got some tasty dressing!

GORGONZOLA DRESSING

1 nice minced piece garlic
½ teaspoon dry mustard
A little pinch salt

¼ cup olive oil
½ cup wine vinegar
3 oz. Gorgonzola cheese

If you've got a blender, throw in everything and blend. If you don't have one (what's the matter, you can't save stamps?), mash everything together with a fork. This dressing you can also make with Roquefort cheese, but Gorgonzola is much cheaper and just as good. This is a good dressing to serve on cold string beans, cannelloni, chick peas or even lettuce.

* NEBISH: on his trip to Italy, he tried to get hotel reservations in Pompeii.

JULIUS CAESAR SALAD
ALLA GAHTKUS*

1 clove garlic, minced	1 teaspoon Parmesan cheese
2 strips anchovy, mashed	A sprig or so of parsley
A pinch pepper & salt	1 raw egg (when you mix
2 tablespoons salad oil	it up, nobody can tell)
2½ tablespoons vinegar	Romaine
4 tablespoons mayonnaise	Croutons (before serving)
(or yoghurt, if you're	
zoftik)	

There are 2 ways you can make this salad. One is to make the salad dressing by mixing good together everything but the croutons and romaine. Some folks feel funny about serving a raw egg and cook it just a few seconds. But, believe me, that's just extra work and extra dishes to wash. Like when you put a raw egg in a malt, who can tell? When you're ready to serve the salad, you'll pour the dressing over the torn romaine leaves and throw in some croutons to help soak up that delicious dressing.

But if you want to be fancy, you can rub a nice size salad bowl with the minced garlic (a wooden bowl is better for this), then mash very nice with a fork the anchovies. Now you'll sprinkle the salt and pepper. Mix it all up and pour on the salad oil, vinegar and mayonnaise (or yoghurt). With a fork you'll give everything a nice few healthy stirs. Now put in the cheese, parsley and that egg. You'll give one more nice mix to everything and for an extra treat, lick the fork before you put it in the sink. Cover the salad bowl and put it in the refrigerator. Later, when you're ready to serve the salad, put the romaine in the bowl with the dressing, throw on the croutons and toss.

You'd better have extra copies of this recipe, because whenever anyone serves this salad, everybody always says, "For this I want the recipe before I leave." The egg you can tell them about at the door when you're saying goodbye.

* GAHTKUS: what Julius Caesar's mother made him wear under his toga on cold days.

27

ARTICHOKE SALAD CON
OLIVIA OLIO*

1 package frozen artichoke
  hearts
A pinch salt
A pinch pepper
2 tablespoons wine vinegar

6 tablespoons olive oil
A little clove garlic, crushed
A pinch sugar
Some romaine

Boil nice the frozen artichoke hearts and put them in the refrigerator, they should get cold. Meantime, you'll mix together all the other things (except the romaine). Now you can take out from the refrigerator the artichokes and put them on a few pieces nice romaine. If there's room in your refrigerator, you'll have the salad on the plates all ready to serve. Pour on the sauce just before you put the salads on the table. This should be enough for about 4 people, who, you'll be sure, like artichoke hearts.

* *OLIVIA OLIO:* Italian chicken *shmaltz*.

EGG & MATZOH DISHES

EGGS DON GIOVANNI
IZZAH GOY*

1 cup tomato sauce	8 slices white bread
1 tablespoon chopped parsley	A little olive oil
A nice pinch garlic powder	8 slices Mozzarella cheese
A pinch salt & pepper	4 nice eggs
½ teaspoon oregano	

Mix nice together in a saucepan the tomato sauce, parsley, garlic powder, salt, pepper and oregano. Now let this simmer for 10 minutes and then put it aside. Take out your baking pan and lay in it 4 slices of the bread. Brush on a little olive oil, put on each piece 2 slices of cheese and spread on the tomato sauce mixture. The other 4 slices bread you'll press out from the center a hole using a water tumbler. Put these on top of the other slices to make sandwiches and also brush with a little oil. Now you can bake in the oven at 325° until the cheese melts. Meanwhile, poach in a little salted water the eggs and when the "sandwiches" are done, put the poached eggs in the little pressed out hole. Serve this to 4 people, nice and hot. But if you're very hungry, you should fix 2 sandwiches per person; and if you're still hungry, maybe you should have eaten out tonight.

* *DON GIOVANNI:* the only one on Grandma's block with a Christmas tree.

OMELET ALLA GRAND
CONCOURSE*

2 tablespoons olive oil
3 medium onions, chopped
1 clove garlic, chopped
1 cup canned drained tomatoes
¾ cup chopped mushrooms

A few pinches salt
A little pinch pepper
1 tablespoon chopped parsley
1 teaspoon oregano
6 nice fresh eggs

In a little saucepan you'll put the onions and garlic and sauté until they get soft. Then you'll put in the tomatoes, mushrooms, salt, pepper, parsley and oregano. Let this simmer for 20 minutes. While you're simmering, you can beat up nice the eggs with a little salt and pepper. When the filling is almost ready you'll put a little oil into a nice large frying pan and make a big omelet. Now put the omelet on a platter and pour on one side the filling. The egg now, you should fold over the filling and cut it up into portions so you can serve. This makes a nice Sunday breakfast for 4 people, especially if you've got company. Serve with or without toasted bagels, depending on what time you're serving lunch.

* *GRAND CONCOURSE:* The Jewish Appian Way.

UM GEPAHTCH KID MATZOH BREI PARMIGIANA*

6 matzohs	A couple pinches salt
1 chopped onion	A little pepper
1 clove garlic, chopped	5 nice fresh eggs
1 tablespoon olive oil	½ cup diced Mozzarella
2 cups tomato sauce	cheese
1 tablespoon parsley, chopped	

Soak first the matzohs in water so they'll be soft. While you're soaking, you can sauté the onion and garlic in the olive oil until they brown a little. Then put them into a saucepan and add the tomato sauce, parsley, salt and pepper. Let this simmer good for 20 minutes. Now you can drain the matzohs by squeezing out from them the water. Mix them together with the eggs, salt and pepper and put half of this mess into an oiled casserole. Sprinkle over this, half the cheese and then the rest of the matzoh mixture. Sprinkle on the rest of the cheese and pour on the top the tomato sauce. Now you'll put the casserole uncovered into a 325° oven and let it cook for 25 minutes. This will be almost as fluffy as a soufflé and will surprise 5-6 people.

* UM GEPAHTCH KID: those snazzy new cars from Detroit with everything from gold plated hub caps to "his" and "her" safety belts.

PASTA & OTHER STARCHES

 ## MANICOTTI CON RICOTTA DI MIA BUBBA*

FIRST, THE SAUCE:

4 tablespoons olive oil
2 cloves garlic, minced
1 medium onion, chopped fine
2 tablespoons chopped parsley

2-1 lb. cans tomatoes
1-8 oz. can tomato sauce
Salt & pepper, you should taste
1 teaspoon sugar
½ teaspoon basil

Sauté in olive oil the garlic, onion, and parsley until the onion and garlic look golden. Then add the rest of the ingredients and simmer uncovered 'til it's thick . . . about 20 minutes.

Now you'll make ready the Manicotti and the stuffing while the sauce cooks. But keep an eye on it, you should stir now and then. You know what they say: "A watched pot cooks maybe a little faster."

NOW THE MANICOTTI:

Cook the Manicotti (which looks like very healthy spaghetti) in a pot boiling salted water, with 1 tablespoon olive oil, so it shouldn't all stick together . . . *only cook 'til it's half-done,* about 12 minutes. (If you forget to do this, you can forget all about it, and fix tuna fish tonight.) Then you should drain and rinse in cold water. Put the Manicotti aside and you're ready for:

34

FINALLY, THE CHEESE FILLING:

1 lb. Ricotta cheese
¼ lb. Mozzarella cheese, sliced thin
¼ cup grated Parmesan cheese

1½ teaspoons sugar
2 eggs, beaten nice
A few pinches salt & pepper

Mix everything together—it won't hurt you to use your hands, but don't forget to beat first the eggs. Fill up the half-cooked Manicotti (one whole box has 12 pieces) with a teaspoon. Pour a little sauce in the bottom of a baking dish or pan and put the filled Manicotti side by side in one row. Now pour some sauce over the Manicotti and then sprinkle lots of Parmesan cheese on top. If you have to make another layer, be sure to put the sauce on top and then some more Parmesan cheese. Put this in an oven heated already to 350° and cook maybe 30 minutes. (The *goyem* make this with a meat filling, too. For that we wouldn't think of even telling you the recipe. You'll have to look someplace else—like maybe the library where the neighbors won't see.)

* *RICOTTA DI MIA BUBBA:* Grandma's cottage cheese she brings to eat when she visits her *goyisha* friends.

RAVIOLI GALITZIANA*

YOU'LL MAKE FIRST THE DOUGH:

1½ cups flour
1 nice fresh egg

A little pinch salt
1 tablespoon water

First you'll pour on a bread board the flour in a little pile. Now with your finger, make a little hole. Beat up nice the egg and drop it in the hole with the salt and the water. Next you should work it with your fingers and maybe a fork until it gets stiff. Then knead it with your hands a little bit. When it's smooth, cover it up and let it stand for 10 minutes. While you're waiting, it's a good idea to look for your rolling pin. It's probably not where you thought it was. Now, after the 10 minutes are up and you've found the rolling pin, you can cut the dough in half and roll each piece so it gets nice and thin.

NOW FOR THE FILLING:

1 cup ground cooked meat
  or chicken
1 fresh egg, beaten up
A few pinches salt
A few pinches chopped
  parsley

½ clove chopped garlic
2 tablespoons bread crumbs
1 tablespoon parve margerine

36

Mix nice together all these things and put a teaspoonful of it on 1 piece of the dough. Keep putting on teaspoonsful 2 inches apart from each other until all of the filling is used. Then you'll take the other piece dough and cover the whole thing up. With your fingers you can press around each little pile of filling so that the dough sticks together and also makes a little square. Now you can cut the squares apart with a little cookie cutter. Make hot a pot water with a little salt in it and when it's boiling good, put in the ravioli and for 10 minutes you should cook and then drain it. We recommend you pour over it the TO-MATO SAUCE ALLA HEIM SHMEEL (see page 46). Some folks would call this *kreplach* . . . but so you should be modern, you call it ravioli. Serves 5, maybe 6 people.

* *GALITZIANA*: the Jewish equivalent of a Sicilian.

LASAGNE SPINACI MAZELDIK*

1 lb. spinach	1 lb. Ricotta cheese
2 cloves garlic, chopped	2 teaspoons salt
3 tablespoons parsley	A few pinches pepper
1 tablespoon basil	1-10 oz. package Lasagne
1 teaspoon oregano	½ cup grated Parmesan cheese
1 cup bread crumbs	
1-1 lb. can tomatoes	½ lb. Mozzarella cheese
1-6 oz. can tomato paste	1 cup tomato sauce

Rinse good the spinach and put in a pot with a little water. Put on the cover and cook for a few minutes until it's done. Then put the spinach with the garlic, 1 tablespoon parsley, basil and oregano altogether in a blender, or chop it good so it's fine. Now mix in the bread crumbs, tomatoes and the tomato paste. Put this on the side so you'll have room to work on the other stuff. Next you'll take the Ricotta and mix in the salt, pepper, and 2 tablespoons parsley. Put this also on the side; in a minute or two you'll need plenty room. On the package Lasagne you'll see some directions on how you should cook. The only thing we can add is you should cook in a large roasting pan so the noodles can stretch out and not break. Also, add a little spoon oil in the water so the noodles they shouldn't stick together. When it's all done, you'll start to put it together. Grease a little bit the bottom of a baking pan and put in a layer Lasagne noodles, then put in a layer of spinach mixture, then a layer of Ricotta, sprinkle on a little Parmesan cheese and some of the Mozzarella cheese in thin slices. Then you'll put on top another layer noodles and start spreading the other stuff like you just did before. Keep doing this until everything is all used up, but make sure you finish up with a layer of the spinach mixture. On top of this, put a little Mozzarella and a cup tomato sauce. (If you didn't listen and you finished up with noodles, it's *your* teeth that'll break. You'll see how hard those noodles can get!) When everything is all put together the right way, you'll pop into the oven and bake for ½ hour at 375°. This will serve 6 average people or 4 people who, "never eat spicy food, but maybe I'll have just a taste."

---

* *SPINACI MAZELDIK*: it's lucky we had the spinach to replace the meat in this recipe; otherwise, there'd be no Lasagne!

 HUMUTZDIK POLENTA SQUARES*

2 tablespoons olive oil
1 clove garlic, chopped
½ cup celery, diced
1 medium onion, chopped
1 quart water

1 cup cornmeal, yellow
2 teaspoons salt
2 or 3 tablespoons Parmesan cheese, optional

Enough parve oleo to dot

Sauté in the olive oil until it's nice and brown the garlic, celery and onion. While this is sautéeing, boil good the water and add slow the cornmeal, mixing all the time so you shouldn't get lumpy. When it's all mixed and smooth, into a double boiler you'll put it together with the sautéed vegetables and the salt. Now cover it up and let it double boil for about ½ hour until it gets thick. When it's thick enough, pour it into a greased 10 x 14 inch pan and let it cool. When it's cool, cut it into 1½ inch squares and sprinkle with the Parmesan cheese. Now dot each square with a little oleo and put it into a 400° oven for 20 to 25 minutes to get a little brown. If you're *fleischig* leave out the Parmesan. It'll still be good. This makes enough polenta for 5 to 6 people, and it's a nice change from potatoes or rice.

* *HUMUTZDIK:* pizza at the Passover table.

40

SHMUTZIK RICE WITH
CHICKEN LIVERS*

1⅓ cups raw rice
1 cup cooked, diced chicken livers
2 medium onions, chopped
2 nice cloves garlic, chopped
1 diced green pepper

3 tablespoons olive oil
3 chopped up scallions
1 tablespoon parsley flakes
Enough salt & pepper so it should taste like something

Cook the rice nice, it shouldn't stick together, but you'll be sure to turn off the fire a little before it's finished. While this is cooking, sauté the onion, garlic and pepper in olive oil until they're nice and brown. Add this to the almost cooked rice. Now you can also add the diced chicken livers, salt & pepper, the scallions and the parsley. Put a little dot here and there with margerine and cover and cook for 15 minutes in a 350° oven. This makes 5 or 6 portions you won't be ashamed of and it's a sneaky way to make the kids eat liver.

* SHMUTZIK: refers to the "scenic" postcards Dave brought back from Naples.

 RISOTTO ALLA SHABBOS GOY*

1 tablespoon olive oil	3 cups vegetable or chicken
1 large onion, chopped	broth
2 ribs celery, chopped	A little salt to taste
1 clove garlic, minced	A pinch or 2 pepper
2 cups raw rice	

Sauté in the oil the onion, celery and garlic until it's a little golden. You'll throw in the rice and make low the fire. Stir this good until the rice turns yellow. Now, you can add the broth, salt and pepper, put on the cover, and cook on a low flame for 30 minutes or until the rice is nice and tender. This will be plenty for 4 to 6 people and it's not as fattening as Potato Kugel.

* *SHABBOS GOY*: the "Friday nighter lamplighter" who knows more Jewish words than you do.

SAUCES

MEAT SAUCE MONA LISENBAUM*

2 tablespoons olive oil	A good few pinches salt
2 cloves garlic, chopped	A pinch pepper
1 cup onions, diced	1 teaspoon oregano
1 cup green pepper, diced	2 nice bay leaves
1 cup celery, chopped	1-6 oz. can tomato paste
1 lb. nice ground beef	1-1 lb. can peeled tomatoes

1 cup dry red wine or water (live it up and use wine!)

First you'll brown with the oil the garlic, onions, celery and green pepper. Then throw in the chopped meat and also let it brown. Mix in all the other stuff and let it cook on a nice low fire for an hour. When it's done, serve on top of spaghetti. This is plenty for 4 or 5 people. Serve with this a big green salad and garlic bread and, you'll see, the kids won't be running off all the time to the corner Pizzeria.

* *MONA LISENBAUM:* Mona Lisa's name before the family left Poland.

MARINARA SAUCE
CRISTOFORO COLOMBO*

2 tablespoons olive oil
2 nice onions, sliced
2 cloves garlic
2-1 lb. cans peeled tomatoes
A few anchovies

A little pinch salt
A little pinch pepper
A pinch sugar
A little pinch oregano
2 ozs. Parmesan cheese

Sauté nice the onion and garlic in the olive oil until it's golden. Take out from the pan the garlic and put in next the tomatoes and simmer for an hour. Then put in the anchovies cut in small pieces, the salt, pepper, sugar and oregano. Cook for 10 minutes more and serve over a pound of cooked spaghetti. Don't forget to sprinkle on the cheese. This will be enough for 4 or 5 people if they don't overdo it.

* CRISTOFORO COLOMBO: my son, the discoverer.

TOMATO SAUCE ALLA HEIM SHMEEL*

2 tablespoons olive oil
3 chopped cloves garlic
3 nice chopped onions
3 tablespoons chopped parsley
2-1 lb. cans tomatoes
1-6 oz. can tomato paste

¼ cup dry red wine
A good few pinches salt to taste
A pinch or 2 ground pepper
1 teaspoon oregano
1 bay leaf

Make hot a saucepan with the oil and cook the garlic and onions until they are soft. Then you'll throw in the rest of the stuff and put the cover on the pot. Now you'll simmer for 2 hours. If the sauce is a little too thin for you, take off from the pot the cover for the last half hour. When it's finished take out the bay leaf and it's ready to serve. It makes about 6 cups and is perfect for *milchidig* spaghetti, all kinds ravioli, or just plain *luckshen*.

* *HEIM SHMEEL*: the Jewish John Doe.

FISH

 ## GEFILLTE FISH FRA DIAVOLO*

8 nice pieces gefillte fish

Is there a *bubba* in the house? Or maybe nearby? If there is, ask her if she would please make the gefillte fish for you. Nobody makes gefillte fish like a *bubba* does. If you're not so lucky, or if *bubba* is in Florida when you decide to make this, you'll find the kind that comes in jars is almost as good, and a lot less trouble. So let's say you already have the fish. Here's what you need to make it FRA DIAVOLO:

2 tablespoons olive oil
3 cloves garlic, chopped
2 cups canned plum tomatoes
2 tablespoons vinegar
1 teaspoon basil

2 tablespoons parsley, chopped
1 teaspoon oregano
¼ teaspoon crushed red pepper seeds
A little salt

Brown good the garlic in the olive oil in a saucepan. Mash up the tomatoes and put together with the garlic and all the other stuff. Be careful when you put the fish in, they shouldn't break. Now you can let the whole thing simmer for 10 minutes and it's ready to serve. Nobody ever serves gefillte fish as a main dish, so you be different. Spaghetti would be very nice with this to cover with some of that good, hot sauce.

* *GEFILLTE FISH*: in every Jewish home there's a *mezuzah* on the doorpost and this in the refrigerator.

FASHTUNKENA FILET
OF SOLE FIRENZE*

1½ lb. filet of sole	¼ teaspoon pepper
½ cup flour	6 tablespoons butter
1 teaspoon salt	2 cloves garlic, minced

Dust good the fish in the flour mixed together with the salt and pepper. Now you can fry it in the butter until one side is a nice golden brown. Then turn it over and get the other side the same color, they should match. Take out from the pan the fish, and put the pieces in a heated serving dish. Add the garlic to the leftover butter in the pan, sauté it for 2 minutes and pour the whole thing over the fish. Now you'll decorate with some parsley and a few wedges lemon, you should be fancy. Serves 4. This, I'll guarantee you, is an easy dish to make, and such flavor you'll pay plenty for when you eat out!

* *FASHTUNKENA:* Venice at low tide.

QVELLING COD FILETS*

A little butter
1 small onion, sliced like paper
¾ cup dry white wine
2 lbs. cod filets (4 pieces)
A little olive oil for brushing

Some Parmesan cheese for sprinkling
Some bread crumbs, also for sprinkling
A little parsley, chopped
2 teaspoons flour
A pinch salt
½ cup milk

Smear light a baking dish with the butter and the onion slices you'll put in, in one layer. Then you can pour in the wine, (also you can take a little sip yourself; it's good for the appetite). Put in the 4 pieces cod and with a little olive oil you'll brush. Sprinkle on some Parmesan cheese and then some bread crumbs. Now top it off with the chopped parsley and the whole thing you'll bake uncovered in a 350° oven for about 20 minutes, or until it flakes nice. Meanwhile, the flour, salt and milk you'll mix together and heat and stir until it gets thick. When the fish is ready, pour the liquid from the baking dish into the flour-milk mixture and you'll cook until the whole thing thickens a little. Pour it over the fish and serve. This is a good dish to serve to your Catholic friends if they should come to visit on Friday. Serves 4 friends if you also fill them up with a nice vegetable, and maybe a salad with one of those cheese dressings.

---

* QVELLING: Mom's pride when she finds out her new daughter-in-law is going to keep Kosher.

FRAYLIKHA FISH STEW*

1 lb. cod
1 lb. flounder filets
1 lb. halibut
1 tablespoon olive oil
1 large onion, sliced
2 cloves garlic, chopped
2 ribs celery, diced
1-1 lb. can plum tomatoes
1-8 oz. can tomato sauce
1 tablespoon lemon juice
½ cup mushrooms

1 package frozen zucchini
1 tablespoon parsley, chopped
1 cup water
1 teaspoon basil
1 teaspoon thyme
A good few pinches salt
¼ teaspoon crushed red pepper seeds
1 teaspoon MSG

First you should remove all the skin and bones from the fish; but don't throw them away—in this recipe, there's no waste. Now cut up the pieces fish into little bite sizes. You can sauté until they're soft the onions, garlic and celery. Put these together with the fish into a large nice looking pot. If you listened and still have the skin and bones from the fish, you'll tie them up in a clean piece cloth, and put in the pot. Now all the other stuff you'll put in also and then cover. Simmer for 20 to 25 minutes. When it's all ready, be sure to throw away the cloth. Imagine what the folks at the table would say if you served them fish skin and bones wrapped up in a wet *shmatah*. Now you're ready to serve with mounds of fluffy rice, and this colorful stew will be enough for 7 or 8 people—and maybe some left for tomorrow.

* *FRAYLIKHA:* describes the day Arnie told the folks he was giving up the Peace Corps to become a doctor.

MEATS

 # FLANKEN PIZZAIOLA ALLA SHMENDRICK*

FIRST YOU'LL NEED SOME BOILED BEEF:

3 lbs. nice beef to boil	A couple sprigs parsley
4 quarts water	A little handful salt
2 stalks celery	A few peppercorns
2 nice onions with cloves stuck in	1 bay leaf
	1 tomato

Put everything together in a pot and bring it to a good boil. Then you'll simmer for 3 hours with the cover on. Take out from the pot the beef and cut it in thick slices. The broth you should strain and put away for minestrone or something. The vegetables you'll throw away, such soaked out things you don't need.

NOW FOR THE PIZZAIOLA SAUCE:

2 tablespoons olive oil	A pinch or two salt
2 cloves garlic, sliced	A good pinch pepper
1-1 lb. can tomatoes	½ teaspoon oregano
1-6 oz. can tomato paste	1 tablespoon parsley

Brown first the garlic in the olive oil. Then put in the tomatoes, tomato paste, salt, pepper, oregano, and parsley. Cook on a medium fire for about 15 minutes. If you boiled the beef maybe yesterday and it's cold, you can throw in the pieces in the sauce and let them get hot together. This is a wonderful new way to serve a piece flanken and it's enough for 4 or 5 people . . . it depends on what time they had lunch.

* *SHMENDRICK:* he invites a date to a formal and takes her there on a subway.

53

GEHACKTA BEEF DI
MAMA MIA*

1 lb. ground beef	¼ cup olive oil
6 thin strips pimiento	2-8 oz. cans tomato sauce
6 slices salami, shredded	2 tablespoons parsley
1 beaten egg	A few pinches oregano
A few pinches salt	A few pinches garlic
A few pinches pepper	powder
A little flour	1 teaspoon sugar

Spread the beef out on a floury board and pat it out until it's about a half inch thick. Now you'll sprinkle on the strips pimiento, and salami. Pour over this the beaten egg and a little salt and pepper. Now roll it up already like a strudel and dust a little flour on the outside. Put the oil in a good size casserole and brown the meat roll on all sides. Be careful how you're handling; it can fall apart very easy. After you brown, you can next pour on the tomato sauce and throw in the parsley and the rest of the "pinches" and sugar. Let it simmer without a cover for a half hour. If the sauce gets a little too thick for you, it's alright to add a little water or even wine if you like. Skim off the fat. Serves 4 people. (If you don't have 4 people to serve, invite in the kids on the front stoop.)

---

* *MAMA MIA:* her name is Giacobbi instead of Jacobs; she makes minestrone instead of chicken soup; and she cooks with olive oil instead of shmaltz.

SALTIMBOCCA ALTE KAHKA*

1½ lbs. very thin veal (in
    3x4 inch pieces)
¼ cup flour
A few pinches salt
A pinch pepper
¼ cup olive oil

A very thin corned beef
    slice for each piece veal
2 hard cooked eggs, halved
4 green olives, pitted
½ cup broth
2 tablespoons sherry

Pound first the veal so it should be good and thin. Now mix together the flour, salt and pepper and dredge in this the veal pieces. Now you can brown these in the olive oil. Don't forget to turn them over and brown both sides. When this is finished, put the pieces into a serving dish and arrange them so they look like something. Now you can put on each piece one of the thin corned beef slices. On 4 of these pieces put on a half egg, and one of the green olives you'll stick on with a toothpick. Now you'll put the broth in the pan you browned in and boil it together with the sherry for 1 minute. Scrape the pan while you're boiling so you'll mix in the little brown pieces in the broth. Pour this sauce over the veal and put the whole dish into a medium oven to warm up. Serve it right away, it shouldn't get cold. Serves 4 people. If it looks too good to eat, just close your eyes and start cutting.

* ALTE KAHKA: "that li'l ole winemaker, me!"

TANTE LEAH'S BRACIOLE
CON CHIANTI*

2 steaks totalling 3 lbs.
A few pinches salt & pepper
Plenty of paprika
13 small or medium mush-
    rooms
 6 small onions
A few thin slices pimiento
¼ cup finely rolled bread
    crumbs

½ cup melted parve marge-
    rine
1 tablespoon boiling water
1 whole raw egg
5 or 6 sliced stuffed olives
¼ cup parve margerine
½ cup flour
1 cup dry red wine

If you're friendly with your butcher, you'll get him to pound
thin the steaks . . . if you're a little shy, you'll pound yourself at
home. Rub in nice some salt, pepper, and plenty paprika. Put
one steak a little bit over the long edge of the other one, so it
looks like one large steak. Slice thin about 5 mushrooms and
make a layer of them on the steaks. Next put a layer of very
thinly sliced onion. Add small slices pimiento (you'll see as you
work why everything has to be so thin). Cover all this with the

bread crumbs. Now you'll beat together the melted margerine, boiling water, and raw egg . . . . and right away you should pour it over the bread crumbs. Place the olives in a row along one long edge of the steak, and begin to roll the meat. If you find you have too much stuff, take out a few things . . . . or maybe you didn't slice some things thin, like you were told. Tie the roll firmly with string. Sprinkle flour on the outside, and brown the roll in ¼ cup margerine. Put 8 mushrooms and 5 small onions in a large casserole dish and sprinkle more salt, pepper, and paprika on everything. Be sure to pour 1 cup of dry red wine in the dish. Cook this for about 2 hours in a 350° oven. Keep your eye on this and peep at it now and then . . . . and baste a little. If the liquid gets low, you'll add a little water. Serves 4 to 5 and is very good with rice, a big salad and garlic bread. Put some Italian music on the phonograph, turn the lights down low, fill the glasses with wine . . . . and you'll think you're in Italy. Drink enough of the wine, and you'll swear you're in Italy!

* CHIANTI: a favorite of the construction men who built the Tower of Pisa, which possibly accounts for its present state.

VEAL ROLLATINI ROMEO
AND JULIET*

½ lb. ground meat
1 nice beaten egg
1 clove garlic, chopped
½ teaspoon MSG
A few pinches salt
1 tablespoon parsley, chopped
1 teaspoon fennel
½ teaspoon anise seed
1 lb. thin veal cutlets
4 tablespoons olive oil

SAUCE:
1 chopped onion
2 chopped cloves garlic
A couple pinches basil
½ teaspoon oregano
A few pinches salt & pepper
1-6 oz. can tomato paste
1 cup tomato sauce
A little dash sherry
1 cup water

Mix together the ground meat, egg, garlic, MSG, salt, parsley, fennel and anise seed. Now the cutlets you'll cut into pieces 3-4 inches square and in the center of each piece put a little of the meat mixture. You can roll each cutlet like a *blintz* and stick in a toothpick so you shouldn't come apart. Put the olive oil into a skillet and brown the rolls all over. While they're browning, throw in the chopped onion and garlic, they should also brown. When this looks done, you can throw in the basil, oregano, salt, pepper, tomato paste, tomato sauce, sherry and water. Let this simmer with the cover on for 30 minutes and it's ready to serve with a nice Risotto to 4 hungry people, they should eat hearty!

* ROMEO AND JULIET: the famous play about the tragic love affair between Romeo Montague and Juliet Caplan, immortalized by William Shaeffer.

GEFILLTE BREAST OF VEAL
AHFTZZA LUCHAS*

1-4 lb. breast of veal with a pocket
½ cup parve oleo
1 onion, chopped
1 clove garlic, chopped
1 cup sliced mushrooms
3 cups bread crumbs
3 tablespoons parsley
A good pinch basil
A good pinch marjoram
1 teaspoon MSG
A little salt and pepper
2 fresh eggs, beaten
Enough water or broth to moisten
A big needle and strong thread so you can sew
A little flour
¼ cup water
¼ cup dry white wine
A little paprika

Sauté in ¼ cup oleo the onion, garlic and mushrooms. Meanwhile, mix together the bread crumbs with the parsley, basil, marjoram, MSG, salt, pepper and beaten eggs. Now you can throw in the onions, garlic and mushrooms. Mix this all together and add enough water or broth to make it nice and moist. You'll stuff the veal and then sew up the pocket with a needle and thread. Sprinkle good the veal with the flour and then brown it in the rest of the oleo in a large roasting pan on the top of the stove. Now add the water and wine, sprinkle the veal with a little paprika, put the cover on and roast it in the oven at 325° for 2 hours. If the weather is chilly, have yourself a small glass *schnapps* while this is cooking. If the weather is warm, drink it on the back porch. When the veal is done, mix in a little flour with the drippings and you'll see what a nice gravy it'll make. This will serve about 5 people or maybe 6, if you slice not too thick.

* *AHFTZZA LUCHAS*: when the maid who's been coming every week for 5 years quits the day before the *Bar Mitzvah*.

VEAL SCALOPPINE ALLA
VIA VENETO*

1½ lbs. veal steak
4 tablespoons flour
A few nice pinches salt
A pinch pepper

2 tablespoons parve margerine
¼ cup beef broth
2 tablespoons sherry
A few slices lemon

When you buy the veal, tell the butcher he should cut it nice and thin and pound it a little bit. Then, if he's not too busy, he can also cut it up in 4 inch pieces. If he's too busy, you'll cut it yourself. Then (when you get home, not in the butcher shop) you can mix all together the flour, salt and pepper and dip in it, the veal. Make sure you cover all over. Melt the margerine in a large frying pan and brown good the veal on both sides. When it's good and brown take it out from the pan and keep it warm. Next, you can pour in the pan the broth and the sherry. Cook this on a high fire and scrape up all the stuff from the bottom of the pan. Let it cook for about a minute and then you can pour it on the veal. Now put on the lemon slices. They look pretty on the dish and they're good to squeeze also. This will make plenty for 4 people. They should live and be well!

* VIA VENETO: Ocean Parkway with sidewalk cafes.

VEAL CHOPS GREPSELLA*

4 nice thick veal chops
1 cup wine vinegar
1 nice large egg
1 cup bread crumbs
¼ cup flour
1 tablespoon chopped parsley

1 teaspoon oregano
1 chopped clove garlic
A few pinches salt and
   pepper
4 tablespoons olive oil

First you'll soak the veal chops in the vinegar for about an hour. Then take them out from the vinegar and dry them good. Now beat up the egg with a little bit water and mix up good together the bread crumbs, parsley, oregano, garlic, salt and pepper. Cover good the chops in the flour, dip them a little in the egg and then with the bread crumbs you'll cover over. Now in a frying pan heat the oil and fry on both sides the chops 'til they're brown. Make a little lower the fire and cover the pan and let them cook for about 20 minutes so they'll be tender. This will serve 4 nibblers or 2 *hahzars*.

* *GREPSELLA*: the first thing out of your mouth after you drink the bi-carb.

 LAMB STEW GEZUNTHEIT*

2½ lbs. lamb	1 teaspoon oregano
2 tablespoons olive oil	½ teaspoon mint leaves
1 large diced onion	A few good pinches salt
2 pieces garlic, chopped	& pepper
1 cup water	½ teaspoon MSG
½ cup tomato sauce	

Trim good the fat from the lamb and into 1½ inch cubes you should cut. Put the olive oil into a heavy pot and brown in it the pieces lamb. Then you can throw in the onions and they can also brown a little. Now add the rest of the ingredients, give it a stir, put on the cover and let it simmer for a half hour or so. When it's done, you can serve it to 4 or 5 people who'll practically be able to cut this with a fork. But maybe you should serve knives, just in case.

* GEZUNTHEIT: the thanks for this blessing is always said through a handkerchief.

SHMAGEGGI POT ROAST WITH WHITE WINE*

2 tablespoons olive oil
2 large onions, sliced
4 lbs. of chuck pot roast
1 cup of canned tomatoes
1 chopped up stalk celery

1 sliced carrot
1 cup of dry white wine
A few pinches each of salt, pepper and basil

In the olive oil you'll fry the onions in a casserole dish until they're golden. Put in the beef, brown it good all over. Now add the vegetables, the white wine, the salt, pepper and basil. Put on the cover and simmer slowly for 3 hours. This is so delicious, you shouldn't know from it . . . and it'll serve 6 people. It's just a suggestion, but if you serve this with the *Broccoli Oy Ah Halairia* on page 72 and a rice dish, everybody'll ask you who catered the dinner.

* SHMAGEGGI: He thinks an audience with the Pope is both of them watching a movie together.

FOWL

CHICKEN CACCIATORE VINO ROSSO MOGEN DAVID*

1 large hen, 4 or 5 lbs.	1-6 oz. can tomato sauce
3 tablespoons olive oil	1-1 lb. can tomatoes
1 large onion, chopped	A pinch salt
3 cloves garlic, minced	A pinch pepper
1 rib celery, chopped	½ teaspoon oregano
1 cup sliced mushrooms	½ cup dry red wine

You'll be sure to cut up the chicken in serving pieces. Then heat the oil in a skillet and sauté the chicken until it's brown. Add the onion and garlic and push them around until they brown a little, too. Now you can add the celery, mushrooms, tomato sauce, tomatoes and the other seasoning. Cook very slowly for about an hour; and then, 5 minutes before you serve, you'll pour in the wine. When the whole thing's done, pour it over noodles or spaghetti and get back on the diet tomorrow! This takes good care of 4 or 5 people . . . if you serve lots of *forshpeisa,* you can maybe squeeze out for 6.

* *VINO ROSSO MOGEN DAVID:* a fancy name for Passover wine.

65

CHICKEN OREGANATE CON HUTZPAH*

½ cup flour	1-3 or 4 lb. chicken, cut up
2 teaspoons oregano	¼ cup olive oil
1 tablespoon parsley flakes	1½ cup sliced mushrooms
2 teaspoons salt	½ cup dry white wine
½ teaspoon pepper	

Put in a clean paper bag the flour, oregano, parsley, salt and pepper. Put in 1 or 2 of the pieces chicken at a time, and give the bag some nice shakes. Don't go crazy with it or you'll find white clouds in the kitchen with chicken flying everywhere. Just shake so all the pieces are covered. Now you can put the olive oil in a large frying pan and brown the chicken all over. When they're browned golden you can put them in a baking dish. Don't throw away the oil, because now you'll put in it the mushrooms and sauté them until soft. Add the wine and scrape all the brown stuff off the bottom of the pan. Pour this on the chicken and put the whole thing into the oven for a half hour at 350°. If the pieces aren't done in a half hour—you'll just leave them a little longer; a few minutes more won't hurt. This will serve 4 or 5 people depending on how long they had to wait for dinner.

* *HUTZPAH:* what Molly had when, just because she went down to a size 18 dress, she bought a bikini.

CHICKEN ALLA NUDNIK*

A nice cut up 3 lb. fryer
½ cup flour
2 teaspoons salt
A little pinch pepper
¼ cup parve oleo

2 cups sliced mushrooms
1 cup chicken broth
1 tablespoon lemon juice
1 teaspoon grated lemon rind

Put the flour, salt and pepper in a paper bag and shake in it a few pieces chicken at a time until each piece is covered white all over. Now you'll heat up the oleo in a big enough casserole and brown in it the chicken on all sides. When the chicken is nice and golden, the mushrooms, chicken broth, lemon juice and rind you'll throw in. Cover the pot and let it simmer for a half hour until the chicken is done. Taste the sauce and if you think it needs, add a little more lemon juice. But don't get too sour—this isn't so good either. This will make plenty for 4-5 people and maybe tonight you'll skip yourself the dessert.

---

* NUDNIK: that persistent door-to-door salesman who couldn't understand why you wouldn't buy a New Testament.

CHICKEN NOODLES TZAZZKI*

1-3 lb. chicken
A few pinches salt
A few pinches pepper
2 tablespoons oil
3 large ribs celery, diced
4 green onions, chopped
1 medium onion, chopped
2 cloves garlic, minced
Some sprigs parsley, or
parsley flakes

1 can ripe olives (without
seeds), cut up in little
pieces
¼ cup cut up mushrooms
1 lb. noodles
1-6 oz. can tomato paste
1 tablespoon lemon juice
1 cup water (or ½ cup
water; ½ cup dry wine)

Boil the chicken in water with some salt & pepper so you'll have maybe a quart of stock. (Later the noodles you can boil in the stock.) The chicken has to cook until the meat is practically falling off the bones. When it cools down—if you hurry, you'll only burn yourself—take the meat from the bones. Sauté until they're tender the celery, onions, and garlic. Now put in the parsley, olives, mushrooms, salt and pepper.

Boil the noodles in the chicken stock until they're "al dente" . . . . this, by the Italians, means if the one who's cooking thinks the noodles are done, they're done. After the noodles have been drained, mix with them the chicken, tomato paste, lemon juice, water and wine, if you're using. Cook in a nice covered pot maybe 45 minutes on low heat . . . and now and then, you'll stir. The whole thing serves 8-10 people. With a nice soup and salad, you don't have to serve anything else. . . . and it's even better the next day.

* TZAZZKI: the "emerald" Moe bought in Naples that turned out to be cut from an old Chianti bottle.

VEGETABLES

❦ GAY IN DRAIRD STRING BEANS*

2 packages frozen "French style" string beans
1 nice onion, chopped
2 chopped pieces garlic
2 tablespoons olive oil
1 tomato, peeled and chopped
2 tablespoons chopped celery
2 tablespoons chopped parsley
1 teaspoon savory
A pinch basil
A couple pinches salt & pepper
2 tablespoons dry white wine

First you should prepare the string beans like the package says. While this is cooking, you can sauté the onion and garlic in the oil until it's a little brown. Then you can throw in the tomato, celery, parsley, savory, basil, and white wine and salt and pepper. Let this simmer good for 10 minutes and give it once in awhile a stir. When the string beans are done, drain from them the water and add them to the sauce that you've just simmered. Mix it all together and serve it good and hot. If you don't have savory on your spice shelf, buy some. It's the secret of the recipe. This has such an exotic flavor, you shouldn't ask! And it makes enough for maybe 8 people.

* GAY IN DRAIRD: what the Garfinkles said when that hotel in Palm Beach used the excuse "all booked up."

❧ EGGPLANT PARMIGIANA LA DOLCE VITA*

1 cup olive oil
1 cup onions, chopped nice
2 pieces chopped up garlic
5 cups drained canned to-
matoes
1 tablespoon parsley
A few pinches salt to taste

A pinch pepper
2 nice large fresh eggs
2 tablespoons flour
2 medium eggplants
1 cup diced Mozzarella cheese
1 cup grated Parmesan cheese

Heat up in a frying pan 3 tablespoons oil and put in the onions and garlic until they're golden. Then you can throw in the tomatoes, parsley, salt and pepper and cook it for 25 or 30 minutes. Don't forget to give it once in a while a stir. While it's cooking you can cut up the eggplant into ½ inch slices and also mix together the eggs and flour into a batter. Now you'll dip each piece eggplant into the batter and fry them in the rest of the oil so they'll get good and brown. When they're all ready, put a layer eggplant into the bottom of a casserole, put on some sauce, then a little of the cheese and then some more eggplant. Keep doing this until you're all used up, and try to make the top layer cheese. If you pay attention to what you're doing, you won't have any trouble. Next you can put it into a moderate oven (350°) and let it bake for 25 to 30 minutes. This will make the cheese melt and make a mess from your casserole, but it's worth it. You should have enough for 5 or 6 people.

* LA DOLCE VITA: a hot pastrami, a sour pickle and thou beside me in the Catskills.

BROCCOLI OY AH HALAIRIA!*

1 bunch broccoli	1 stick margerine
A pinch salt	1 tablespoon lemon juice
1 teaspoon anise seed	1 teaspoon capers

First you'll clean good the broccoli and put it in a pot. Add an inch of water and the salt and the anise seed. Now you can steam it for 20 minutes. Meanwhile, you should melt the margerine and add the lemon juice and capers. When the broccoli is ready, put it in a nice serving dish, pour over the sauce and serve it to 4 people. Believe me, too many people just cook broccoli and serve it with nothing on it and it lies there like it's sad. This, we promise, will make happy broccoli.

* *OY AH HALAIRIA!*: street cleaner's lament after a festival on Mulberry Street.

 ## BUPKAS BAKED CAULIFLOWER*

1 nice head cauliflower	½ cup chopped canned mush-
2 tablespoons butter	rooms
2 tablespoons flour	¼ cup bread crumbs
1 cup milk	1 tablespoon parsley, chopped
A few pinches salt	2 tablespoons Parmesan
A pinch pepper	cheese

Boil the whole cauliflower in salted water for 20 minutes. When it's ready, you'll break it up into small sections and put them into a baking dish. (Cauliflower looks so pretty when it's served in a red baking dish. If you have one, use it . . . . if not, don't run out and spend so easily.) Now melt the butter and mix in the flour until it's smooth. Pour in slow the milk and stir on a low fire until it gets thick. When this happens, you can throw in the mushrooms and parsley, together with the salt and pepper. Mix this all together and pour it over the cauliflower. On top of this, sprinkle the bread crumbs and then the grated cheese. Bake this at 375° for 20 minutes and serve to 4 skinny people who "need a little meat on their bones."

* *BUPKAS*: what you tipped the waiter in Milan who spilled Chianti on you.

 STUFFED CABBAGE VIA SHMATAH*

1 large cabbage	1 teaspoon basil
2 onions, minced	2 tablespoons pine nuts (Pignoli)
1 lb. ground meat	
2 tablespoons olive oil	1½ teaspoons salt
1 cup cooked rice	A dash pepper
1 teaspoon marjoram	

FOR THE SAUCE YOU'LL USE:

1-6 oz. can tomato paste	¼ cup or a nice handful raisins
½ cup water	
¼ cup wine (dry red)	½ teaspoon salt
2¼ tablespoons brown sugar	3 tablespoons lemon juice

Put the head cabbage in about 2 inches boiling water and leave about 8 minutes. After you drain it, you'll sauté the onions and you'll brown the meat. This way you'll get rid of the extra fat in the meat. Now you'll mix the onions and meat with the rice, majoram, basil, nuts (if you found them at the grocery), and

74

1½ teaspoons salt, and pepper. Now put a leaf of the cabbage on the table and put about 3 heaping teaspoons mixture at the bottom of the leaf; you'll be able to tell better how much you'll need for each leaf. (Your cabbage may be bigger than my cabbage.) Fold the bottom of the leaf over once at the core end of the leaf. Fold both sides of the leaf toward the center and roll up. Just the way the roll is now, is the way it should be put in the pot (loose end down). If it makes you happier you can use toothpicks, but you don't really need them. Place the rolls in a casserole pot—a good size one.

For the sauce, you'll combine the tomato paste, water, wine, sugar, lemon juice, raisins and ½ teaspoon salt. Pour this over the cabbage rolls and turn on the television. (While the set's warming up, if you have any leftover veal or beef bones, throw them in, too.) Now you'll cover and simmer for 1-1½ hours, depending on how good the show is.

* VIA SHMATAH: a street in Rome where they sell second hand clothing.

MISHIGOYEM MUSHROOMS CON VINO BLANCO*

1 lb. small mushrooms
3 tablespoons olive oil
1 cup tomato sauce
1 cup dry white wine

1 tablespoon parsley
2 cloves garlic, chopped fine
Salt and pepper, to taste

Put the mushrooms whole in a nice looking casserole. Pour in olive oil, tomato sauce, wine, parsley, garlic, salt and pepper. Now you'll give a few careful stirs to get everything mixed nice, cover, and put it in a 350° oven for about ½ hour. This dish you'll find very quick to make, and you'll like it. It serves maybe 4 people if they don't make *hahzars* of themselves.

* *MISHIGOYEM:* they think *Bar Mitzvah* is the name of an Israeli ranch.

DESSERT

SHIRLEY DE MEDICI'S RUM ICE CREAM*

4 egg yolks	1½ cups whipping cream, you'll whip
4 tablespoons sugar	
3 egg whites	¼ cup rum

Beat the egg yolks and sugar together long enough so they're nice and thick. (If you have an electric beater your arm won't be so tired.) In a separate bowl you'll beat stiff the egg whites. Now into the beaten yolks and sugar, fold the whites and whipped cream. After that's done, stir in the best part of all—the rum. Put it all in whatever fits nicely in your refrigerator and freeze it for at least 3 hours. This dessert serves 10 people; and if you're making it you better invite over 10 people or you'll be eating such calories all week and smell like you've been drinking rum all week!

* SHIRLEY DE MEDICI: (née Schwartz—'twas on the Isle of Capri that she met him.)

GELATIN CHEESE CAKE
NOSHEREI*

3-3 oz. boxes different colored Kosher gelatin	½ cup candied fruits & peels
1 lb. Ricotta	2 tablespoons sugar
1-3 oz. package cream cheese	1 teaspoon vanilla

Mix up each package gelatin separately like the box says. Now take a loaf pan (about 11 x 5 x 3), pour in the first color and let it set nice. Meanwhile, you'll mix up together the Ricotta, cream cheese, candied fruits and peels, sugar and vanilla. Now smear half of this on the first layer gelatin. Be careful to keep it at least a half inch away from all the sides so it shouldn't squish out later. Now pour on the next layer gelatin and let this set good. Put on the rest of the Ricotta mixture the same way and then the last layer gelatin. Chill this so everything gets nice and firm and when you're ready to serve, dip the pan in some hot water for a few seconds and then turn it quick upside down on a plate. Slice it up to serve as many people as you need for, (at least 12). If you use red and green gelatin, that with the white cheese filling and you'll have the colors of the Italian flag!

* NOSHEREI: this took the place of cigarettes when Nathan quit smoking. Now they call him "Fat Nat."

BOW-TIES CON AH TRINKELLA SCHNAPPS*

¼ lb. butter
3 egg yolks
2 whole eggs
1 tablespoon sugar
A little pinch salt
2 oz. whiskey

1 teaspoon vanilla extract
2 cups flour
A pot hot oil
A sprinkle can with powdered sugar

Cut first the butter into the egg yolks and eggs. Then add the sugar, salt, whiskey and vanilla. Now mix in the flour slowly and knead it a little bit. When this is done put it into the refrigerator for a half hour. While you're waiting and if the whiskey bottle is still out, pour yourself a little drink. A person that works in the kitchen as hard as you do deserves a glass *schnapps* once in a while. When the dough is through chilling, cut into 4 pieces and roll each piece on a floury board until its very thin. Then you can cut these pieces into strips 6 to 8 inches long and 1 inch wide. Take each piece and tie a little knot in it. You can fry them in the hot oil until they get a healthy golden color. Take them out from the oil and drain. Now sprinkle on the powdered sugar and they're ready to serve. Makes 25 to 30 pieces and they practically melt in your mouth!

* *AH TRINKELLA SCHNAPPS*: this is what made getting a cold fun when you were a kid.

80

ANISE COOKIES ZOL ZEIN MIT GLICK*

3 cups flour	½ cup parve margerine
2 teaspoons baking powder	2 fresh eggs
½ cup sugar	¼ cup milk
A pinch salt	A handful anise seed

Mix together the flour, baking powder, sugar and salt. Now, if you're not so fussy, you'll mix in with your hands, the shortening. Then beat up the eggs and mix them in also. Pour in the milk and mix the whole sticky thing together until it looks smooth and forms a ball. Roll out the dough nice and thin and cut into cookies with a cookie cutter or the edge of a drinking glass. Sprinkle a little anise seed on each cookie and press the seeds in with your hand. The anise seed gives a little tiny taste of licorice. Now you can bake them on an ungreased baking pan in a 350° oven until they're browned a little, about 15 minutes. This will make 30 to 40 cookies, you and the kids will be nibbling for a week.

* *ZOL ZEIN MIT GLICK:* My goodness she's ugly! but you should both live and be well. . . .

CAFFE ESPRESSO SIGNORE DI HADASSAH*

To make good Italian coffee you need French roasted coffee. But you'll look first, you might find Italian roasted coffee at the grocery store in your neighborhood, or even in somebody else's neighborhood. Either one will do because they're both very black and ground very fine. If you want to get real fancy, you can buy an Italian *caffettiera*, which is an Italian coffee maker. . . . but the old drip coffee pot is O.K., too.

FOR OLD DRIP COFFEE POTS:

Boil 4 cups water.
Pour over 5 tablespoons coffee in the top of the pot, and let it drip.
Serve it in a little cup with a nice twist of lemon.
This makes about 8 small cups.

CAPPUCCINO

The experts say this you don't serve after a meal—only between meals and for breakfast. If it makes you feel better to serve it with bagel and lox, so serve! But it tastes just as good after a meal. So who needs rules?

For this you make like for the *espresso* only on top you put a tablespoon of hot cream or hot foamy milk or even whipped cream and a little sprinkle of cinnamon. The way this coffee gets its name is that it's supposed to be the color of the robes the Cappuccine monks wear. (Look—*everybody* can't be Jewish!)

* CAFFE ESPRESSO: what the ladies of Hadassah served with sponge cake to Marc Antony and his troops after the conquest of Egypt.

INDEX

83